SOUL COLLECTION

Soul Collection

VICTORIA KENT

Author

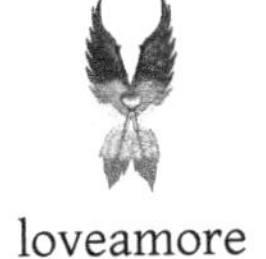

loveamore

To my family.

To life yet to be
explored,
discovered and
experienced.

CONTENTS

FOREWORD

This is a book of poems by the soul for the soul. May you enjoy reading them, feeling them, experiencing the words, the emotions, the feelings as much as I enjoyed writing them. From my heart to yours with curiosity, wonder, love and joy may you be blessed, and your day bring you all the possibility it holds.

To love and love more.

To rise we must fall and when fallen
we will rise

Falling

It is not the critic who counts;
not the man who points out how
the strong man stumbles, or
where the doer of deeds could
have done them better. The
credit belongs to the man who is
actually in the arena, whose face
is marred by dust and sweat and
blood; who strives valiantly; who
errs, who comes short again and
again. —Theodore Roosevelt

~ 1 ~

alone and strong
in the heart belongs
seeds of tomorrow
planted today
in the game we play
moments we choose
to win or lose
to survive or die
to fail or try
it's all in our mind
so love and be kind

~ 2 ~

forgive what was once wrong
release hurt you're holding on
it is not worth the pain
the angst and the shame
so strong and showing
the inner power of knowing
the amazing strength you have
to give and not expect back

~ *3* ~

no one asks why
a child doesn't cry
when in pain
or devoured by shame
silence is golden
that is the key
to keeping things hidden
so people can't see
the secrets that burn
tearing you down
buried deep inside
covered up frowns
the sound of the voice
small and unheard
never revealing
what occurred

~ 4 ~

today I woke with such joy
in my heart
excited for a day
to play my part
then people got involved
clouds form overhead
time to go climb
back into my bed
sometimes I get lonely
sometimes it's so hard
sometimes it's important
to protect a fragile heart

~ 5 ~

driving my car
into that tree
it would all stop
I would be free
that was a thought
I had long ago
when life was hard
but I didn't show
life got hard again
these thought though
did not begin
now I see
the wonder of the tree
the sky sun and stars
what I could be
I now know the bullet
left on my desk
was nothing more
than a spiritual test
it is okay to fall down
just get right back up
rain and hail
are not a fail

~ 6 ~

who isn't damaged
who thinks they are whole
living an illusion
head in a hole
who hasn't been hurt
or doesn't have wounds
who hasn't woke crying
beneath the silvery moon
who hasn't built walls
or chained their own heart
who hasn't given up
on a brand new start
who hasn't felt fear
or rejection or pain
especially when you know
there is so much to gain
who hasn't felt doubt
and run till you drop
and gone without
hoping the feelings would stop
who hasn't wanted more
dreamed big for their life
wanting to break free
of what hasn't been right
we are all the same

so tender deep down
just wanting to be
loved and found

~ 7 ~

we live a story told
not knowing lies we've been sold
throughout the generations
causing fear and stagnation
the hero's through time
broke free from their minds
to explore search and know
adventure teach and show
against the societal grain
pushing forward beyond shame
for what we desire
a life that will inspire
it is there if you dare
to live and not compare
rising up strong
to go further go beyond
the words we hear
and break the bonds of fear

~ *8* ~

we all have battles
hills to climb
they give us character
they help us to find
what really matters
the moments we share
with beautiful people
for whom we care
the animals in our lives
who help us to love and thrive
the sun set and the sun rise
the heart in a message
you are so glad to get
the well wishes
someone has left

~ *9* ~

pain, pain, pain
dripping in shame
memories raging
nightmares awakened
childhood lost
and forsaken
pain, pain, pain
sweet bitter rain
pouring on skin
raging within

$\sim 10 \sim$

some go too soon
some try to go
everyone's story
is their own
the hand you are dealt
the choices you make
become your song
the story you make

~ 11 ~

feelings are seeds sowed
waiting for the sun to grow
warm attention
golden light
it all went away
one dark night

~ *12* ~

emerging tears
from yester years
fall from my face
with such sweet grace
a heart it heals
and learns to feel
with such delight
as it soars and takes flight

~ *13* ~

of days gone by
tears I cried
I grew strong
sang my song
blazed my trial
from whence I hail
from where I come
I must go
to lay in peace
in fields of snow

~ 14 ~

words bumbling tumbling
thundering about
noisy words
I want to shout
I open my mouth
no noise comes out

~ *15* ~

the rage of emotions
tamed and contained
the mask so well prepared
and forcibly sustained
an image to be seen
calm mature and serene
who could possibly tell
the inner screaming hell

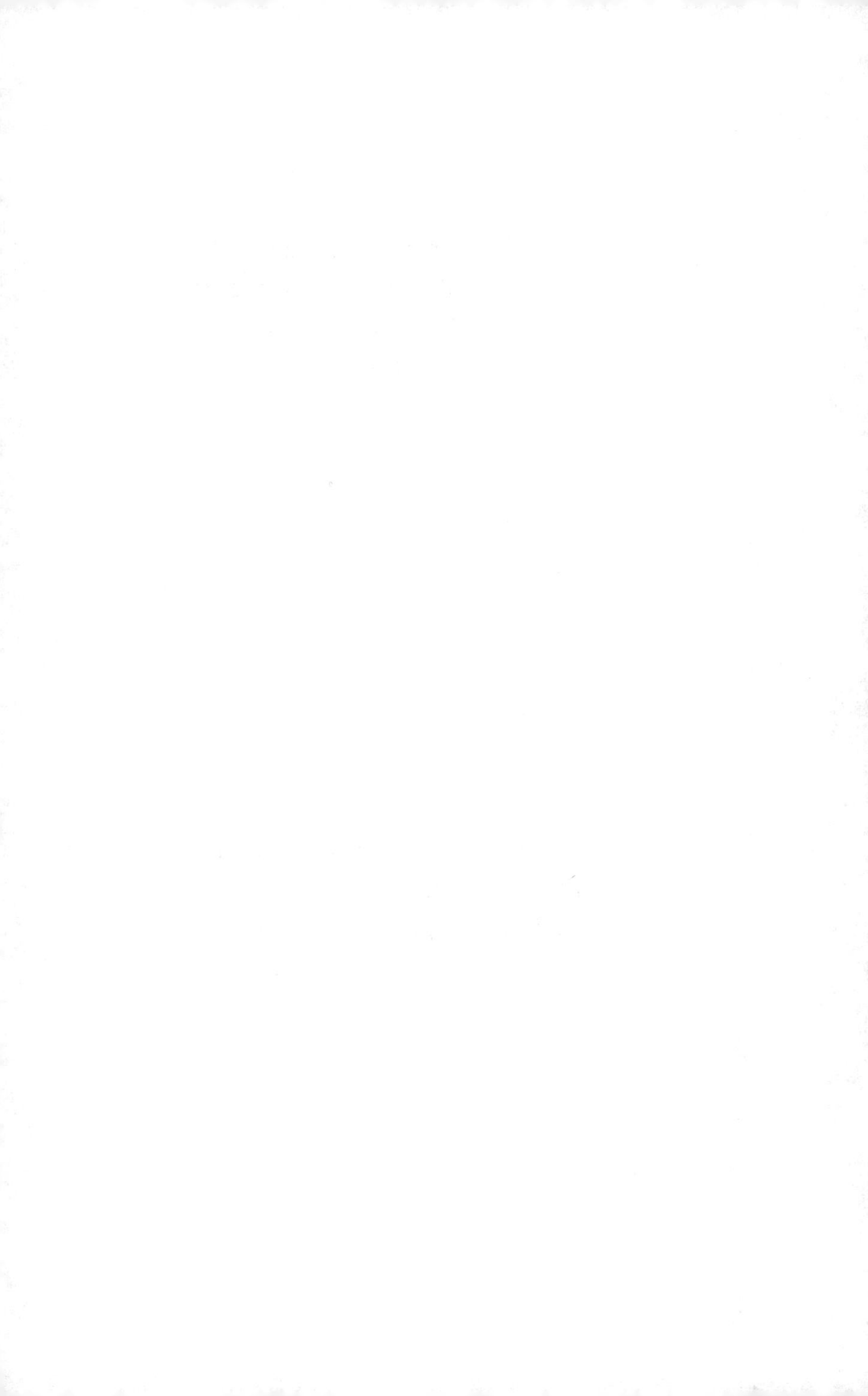

Each day the sun returns each
day is something new, so today
ask yourself, what are you going
to do?

Rising

Imagination is more important
than knowledge. Knowledge is
limited. Imagination encircles
the world.   —Albert Einstein

~ *16* ~

the suns glorious glow
turns up puts on a show
as life wakes and begin to start
another day to play your part
maybe break free the chains
release the hate release the pain
in this story be the one
who sings their own unique song
a brave and courageous act
a predestined bet and pact
to only be true to you
and let each day feel so new

~ *17* ~

the moment in a day
the note in a song
all a part to play
they all belong
each and every
one of us
is a second in time
each of us bringing
a unique
rhythm and rhyme

~ *18* ~

gratitude is the attitude
I want to see
flowing with life
in a river of chi
the suns new day
light up the way
for joy and fun
each new day begun
who am I?
who would you be?
immersed and alive
with gratitude's glee

~ *19* ~

bands of gold will not hold
the heart that can't be tamed
words of doubt raised in shout
the soul they can't contain
flames ignite from the smallest spark
life it turns and arcs
shadow light no wrong it's right
darkness brings out spirits highlights
you and me rise to be
inspiration for the world to see

~ 20 ~

if I only had one day to live
24 hours in which to give
I'd tell of the beauty I see
in all living beings alive and free
I'd tell of the feelings
I kept hidden inside
the love that I felt
that I continue to hide
I'd dance in the rain
sing in the sun
let go all the pain
let my heart run
laugh at more things
especially myself
I'd let people know
they are our true wealth
that it's okay
we can all just be
that is the true essence
of living a life free

~ *21* ~

in beauty we lie
we dream we wake
decisions for love
are ours to make
through closed eyes
blinded by light
give in to joy
give up the fight

$$\sim 22 \sim$$

a new start a new day
anything can come your way
an inspiration an idea
a loving soul to hold dear
creativity and natures glory
tells a wonderous story
where the universe is my wife
and fantasies come to life
she has my back and cares for me
making sure my dreams are free

~ *23* ~

together we are stronger
our focuses combined
life energies and forces
enhanced and entwined
working as a unit
synergy as we go
our family is stronger
to the world it shows

$$\sim 24 \sim$$

a new day
golden light
what blessings will come
what new insights

~ *25* ~

a warrior heart
a warrior mind
to be generous
beautiful and kind

~ *26* ~

leaves rustling birds singing
another glorious day
clear blue oceans dolphins swimming
this is our blessed way

~ 27 ~

blank canvas to create
moonlit dreams it can make
dream it, live it, believe it, now
the wonder in the moment, how

live out loud
loud and proud
of who you are
coming so very far
through the trials
through the pain
seeking rainbows
in the rain

~ 29 ~

busy days and lazy nights
shadows stretch without the light
slow down, wake up
let's shake our way of thinking up
words are missiles
powered by thoughts
direct them wisely
or face the court
justice is blind
but consciousness see's
what's right and wrong
the wood through trees
take a minute from each day
invest it wisely produce the hay
feeling good and sharing light
so shadows stay away tonight

$$\sim 30 \sim$$

there is nothing I want
nothing I need
except for happiness
except for peace

Searching for truth that can
only be found in the inner realm
of you.

E

x

p

l

o

r

i

n

g

When you get all you want and
you struggle for self, and the
world makes you king for a day,
then go to the mirror and look at
yourself and see what that man
has to say. — Dale Wimbrow

~ *31* ~

from within I begin to see
the completion
the awakening of me
of passions hidden
deep down
suddenly aroused
things not experienced
now come into existence
drawn by my mind
seen in my dreams
like hidden aspects of life
now seen

pathways unseen yet dreamed
fill a mind redeemed
from nothing to nothing
born crying, striving, trying
forever working applying
new knowledge and ideas
new perspectives to dry tears

~ *33* ~

peaceful gentle steps
leave no harsh marks
on the dearest
and most loved hearts

$$\sim 34 \sim$$

within passions inner fight
breathes hope love and light
to be seen to be bright
to be the one there each night
a star in someone's eyes
there to comfort inner cries
to become a shining sun
stand and stay and never run
to trust the power and the might
to be the soft voice of right
intuitions powerful embrace
will be my heart's Amazing Grace

~ *35* ~

my mind wonders
far and wide
to the furthest reaches
to where it hides
from what I came
to where I go
wonders around
in its own space of flow

~ *36* ~

connecting to my soul
trying to become whole
pieces of me long lost
buried at what cost

$$\sim 37 \sim$$

unto you I Am
woven with a plan
of mysteries yet dreamed
of wonders not yet seen
into me I wonder
for this world I must ponder

~ 38~

overwhelm my senses
shatter my defenses
you are the beginning
and end of me
through my soul
you see

within the inner realms
worlds twist and turn
imagination cannot detain
realities drowned in toxic rain
minds taken dreams dissolved
people made to fit a mould
expand beyond what you see
to fly and be truly free

~ *40* ~

to sing a song
a bird might sing
to swim in ocean
where dolphins swim
to climb a tree
that monkeys climb
to call this planet
home and mine
we share this world
with so many
and for each and all
there is plenty

$$\sim 41 \sim$$

can you forgive
that I left
like a thief in the night
I crept
stealing my own sanity
it was my vanity
tearing me down
insecurities drown
what I value most
I burn and roast

ocean friend
ocean foe
I watch you
as you come and go
pleasure pain
all combined
within a saltiness
Divine

mirror mirror
reflect back to me
the dreams of who
I hoped I'd be
the lover the fighter
the painter the poet
all of it there
I just didn't know it
how to grasp
the hopes and dreams
break free the binds
rip open the seams

~ *44* ~

let the inside out
the outside in
such a simple concept
so let's begin

~ 45 ~

the inescapable language
of a dimensional rhyme
comes a random thought
or two of mine
the hearts true fire
is a space to relate
associate and recreate
what once was
what could be
the essence the soul
of you and me

Up, up and away to embrace a brand new day.

Soaring

If you can trust yourself when all men
doubt you ... If you can dream and not make
dreams your master ... If you can think and
not make thoughts your aim — Rudyard
Kipling

~ 46 ~

tomorrow you will see
how great it is to be
surfing your own high
exploring who, what, why

~ 47~

walk your path
walk your truth
within your heart
you'll find the proof
that love is
the answer
love is the key
love is the secret
that sets us free

~ *48* ~

to live in wonder
to live in awe
a soul explored
to see the beauty
to feel the sound
of magic all around
to know your truth
with no proof
to stand your ground
through each round
is joy and peace
a past released

~ 49 ~

don't judge a book
by it's cover
there is always
much more to discover

$\sim 50 \sim$

know what is true
know what is real
how do you know
it is what you feel
truth becomes truth
when let in
it's where pain ends
and where love begins

~ 51 ~

if we create who we are
and we are who we create
then who is the prisoner
with the key to the gate
if we attract what we need
and need what we attract
what is the lesson
to be learned in that
if our words are our thoughts
and our thoughts are our words
then we risk a mind
that is easily disturbed
if love is the answer
and the answer is love

~ *52* ~

let my strength
be your strength
my courage
your courage
when you are down
and feel discouraged
look to me
for all you can be
within the mirror
is where you will see

~ *53* ~

what happens when
a force of nature
meets an
insurmountable object
interesting question
interesting subject
pride and ego
crumble to love
as people raise
up and above

~ 54 ~

no soul is perfect
no heart complete
until they seek the truth
of what makes them beat

~ *55*~

yesterdays tomorrows
never come
with the rising and setting
of each new sun
time is endless
or so it seems
until it disappears
in unspoken dreams

~ 56 ~

I am unique to me
someone no one else can be
I am alive to be living
gifts only I am given
I am a child who plays
adult games my own way
I am born
and I bleed
to rise keep going
and succeed

~ 57~

I see beauty in the sunset
as it kisses the sea goodnight
I see beauty in the swaying trees
they live in such peace and ease
I see beauty in the cloudy skies
offering heaven to my eyes

$$\sim 58 \sim$$

transformation expectation
intense reimagination
meant to be awakened
meant to be shaken
roam and explore
life beyond your door

~ 59~

birds sing on cloudy days
the sun lights up the haze
the grass gets greener
a soul as a dreamer
of days in the sun
laughing and fun
flowers face the rain
releasing droughts pain
water it flows
life now grows
the bush on fire
full of passion and desire
blacken in despair
thriving in repair
new growth appears
darkness disappears
the clouds the sun
the rain the seasons
all here for
specific reasons
never forget who you are
how you have come so far
to sing on cloudy days
drink in the suns warm rays
that meant you would survive

to one day shine and thrive

watch me rise
watch me fall
watch me try
to give it all
I did the best
I thought I could
dirty face
marred with blood
dream in time
dream together
nothing can stop
what is together

*From my
heart to
yours, thank
you.*

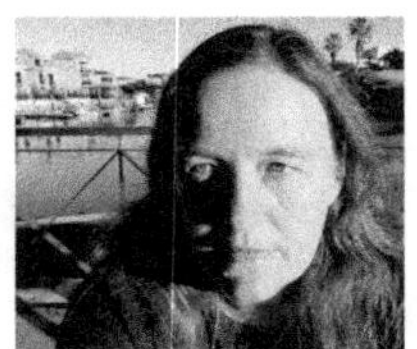

Vicky is a poet, philosopher and writer. She was the first female train driver on the Western Australian public transport network and works as an instructional designer, most recently on the project for the largest robot train in the world.

Volunteering as a counsellor and energy healer she has studied past life regression, EFT, NLP, Reiki, Huna and many other forms of healing and spirituality.

Sharing knowledge and information is a passion for Vicky and she enjoys being able to use mediums such as poetry, art and photography to expand knowledge and understanding.

Book Cover photo also by Victoria Kent

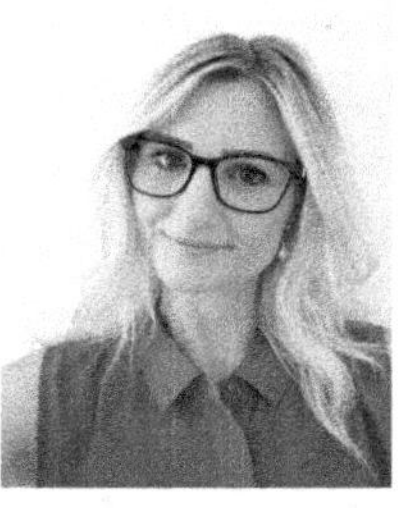

Art by Kelly Williams

The loveamore logo is original artwork from artist Kelly Williams.

Kelly Williams is best known for her colourful, detailed and realistic artworks. The West Australian artist, who is also a TV news reporter, creates bespoke artworks in a variety of mediums.

Kelly has been commissioned to illustrate children's books, paint custom pet portraits, design business logos, create tattoos and transform memorable moments (captured in a photograph) onto paper or canvas.

From a small Country WA town called Wongan Hills, Kelly has grown up being surrounded by beautiful landscapes, people and animals. Now she attempts to convey such beauty through her artwork.

Links to our social media accounts if you would like
to explore our work further

**loveamore
instagram**

**loveamore
facebook**

Art by Kelly
Williams
instagram

www.ingramcontent.com/pod-product-compliance
Lightning Source LLC
Chambersburg PA
CBHW051005050726
47592CB00007B/2715